The BOOK OF JUNIPER

new poems by
TOM PAULIN

drawings by
NOEL CONNOR

BLOODAXE BOOKS

ISBN: 0 906427 16 9 (ordinary edition)
       0 906427 17 7 (limited edition of 25 numbered copies
                      signed by poet & artist)

First published 1981 by
Bloodaxe Books
P.O. Box 1SN
Newcastle upon Tyne NE99 1SN

**The publisher acknowledges the financial assistance
of the Arts Council of Northern Ireland in the publication
of this volume.**
The publisher also acknowledges the financial assistance
of Northern Arts.

Printed in Great Britain by
Tyneside Free Press Workshop Ltd, Newcastle upon Tyne.

THE BOOK OF JUNIPER

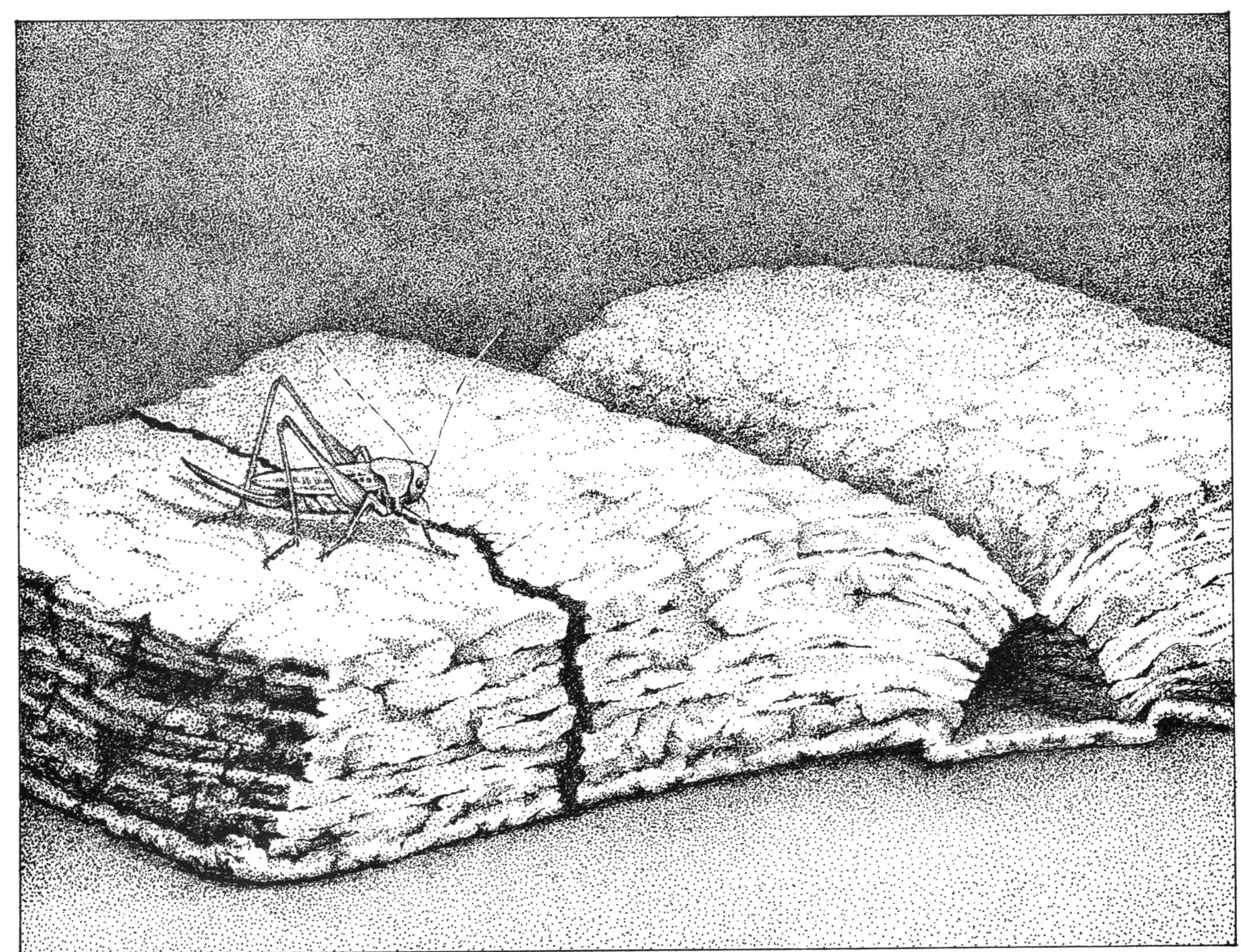

Cinnamon Stick

Like a ghost in a gaberdine
the mnemonist comes hunching
over the smooth grass: oh, he breathes,
I hear psalms in the suburbs;
behold those virgin players
in a drift of light. Lazy
butterflies, they are, white flipflops
dancing on the bouncy green;
their blancoed grace, it bobs and spins
in a pure civil playing. How
this flutters above the haycocks.
I am a chalk man, but; I rise
smoothly from my tomb of vellum,
its sigil a lavender sprig
on a pumice glans: my dreams
web through private libraries
of ancient erotica, pungent
as dolphins anchored on a wave
of bay leaves. I am the nephew
of another nephew, and my
tobacco rhetoric must creak
a dusty music from my lust.
Only Christ, the spirit of the forms,
shivers the surface like a shoal
of fry. He will not answer me;
and I must lay this body down
like a brown whiskered nightjar
shadowing bark and perished leaves.

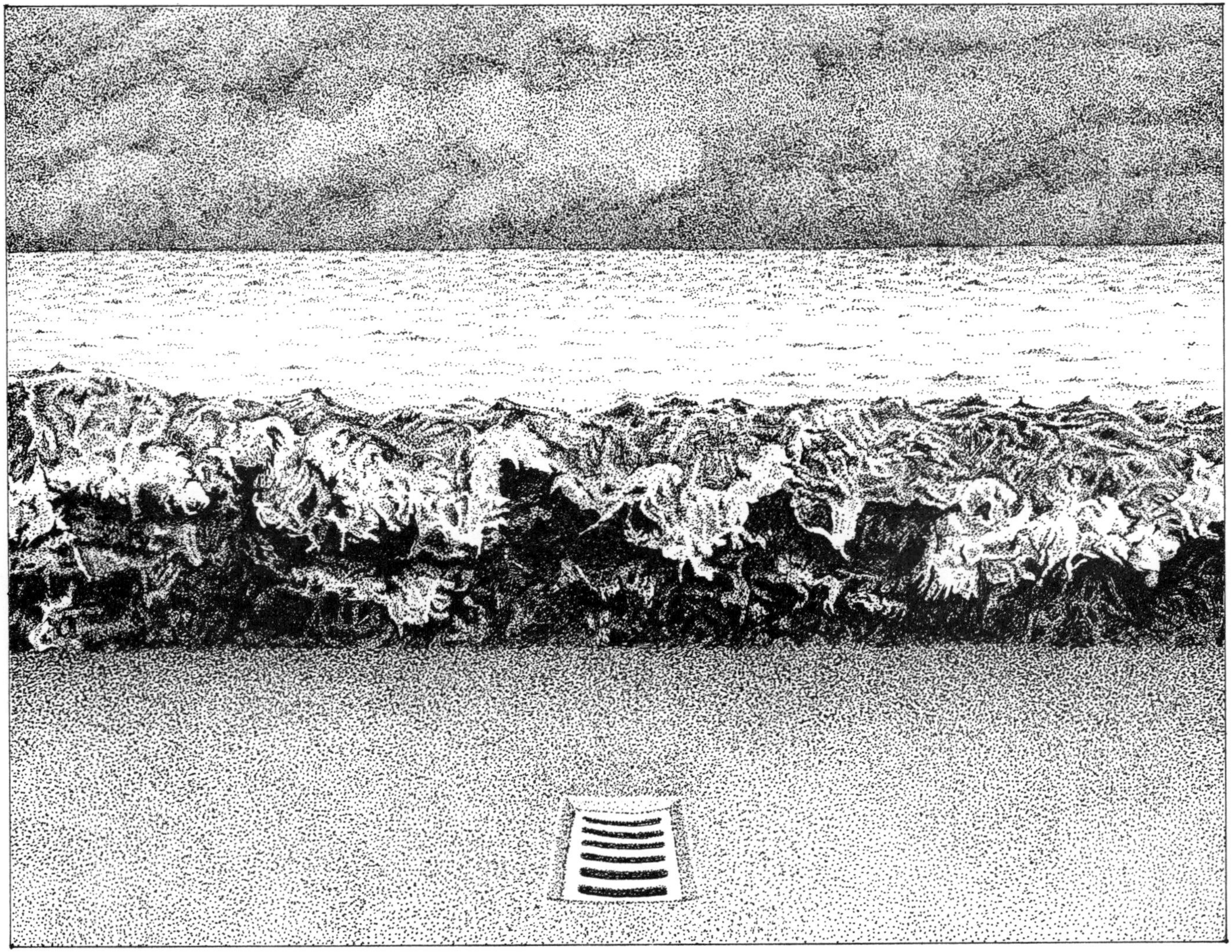

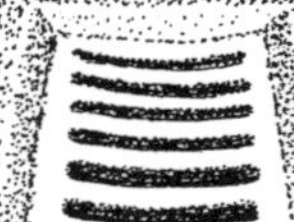

Ceremony on the Border

I see the women come walking
From the town of the white river-meadow.
Their eyes are a silk fragrance;
Their ritual must appease
The squat god, Terminus.

One is shy and delicate
As she carries a bowl of wine;
And another, in the spirit's beauty,
Will transfigure the hard god
With honey on a green leaf.

He hunches at the stone bridge,
The crude lord of limits
In his blocked sangar. His raw
Fur is grey and hackled,
His broody vigilance

The shadow of all judgement.
Rain and lichens
Have weathered him, and now
He squats like an institution.
Useful, half-wise, no longer young.

Honeyed wine and spicy cakes,
A fluid light and a fine
Twist of air—a song is rising
To a gold-bellied sail
That takes, takes and quickens us.

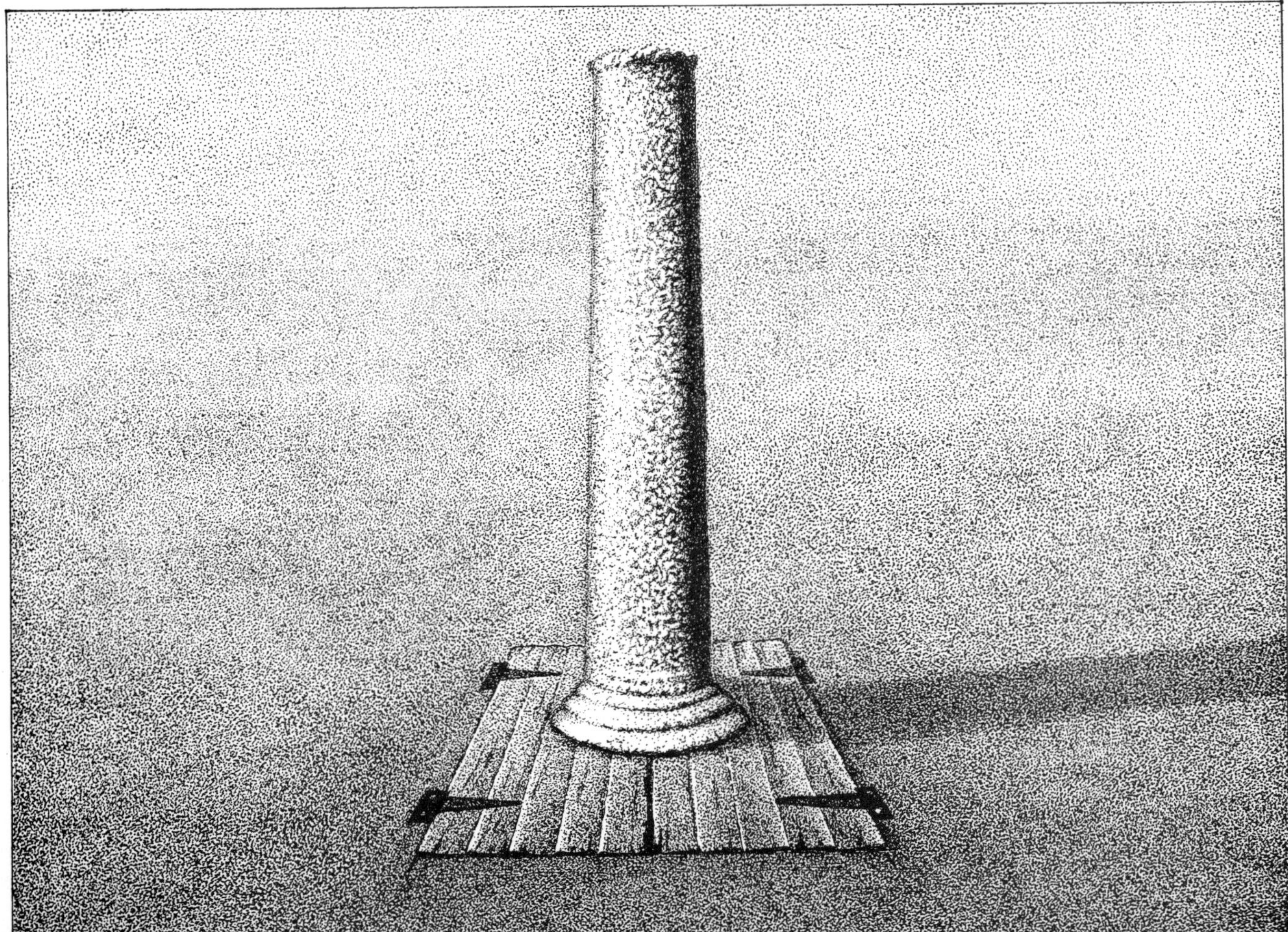

As a White Lodge in
a Garden of Cucumbers

Voluble in a slum,
in a garlic opera
where paper roses
fall from a tarnished ceiling
and the room smells
of roasting ptarmigan,
capsicums, and songs
juicy as peaches,

these careless lovers
have forgotten honesty,
that salt anguish
on a bruised coastline.
It is time, they sing,
to praise the surface,
the pure and twisting
figure of eight that curves

the sun within itself.
They strip to irony
and clever laughter
in a comedy of oil.
Hilarious, his prong;
what a scream her fanny is;
though the boreal teacher
asks, why aren't they serious?

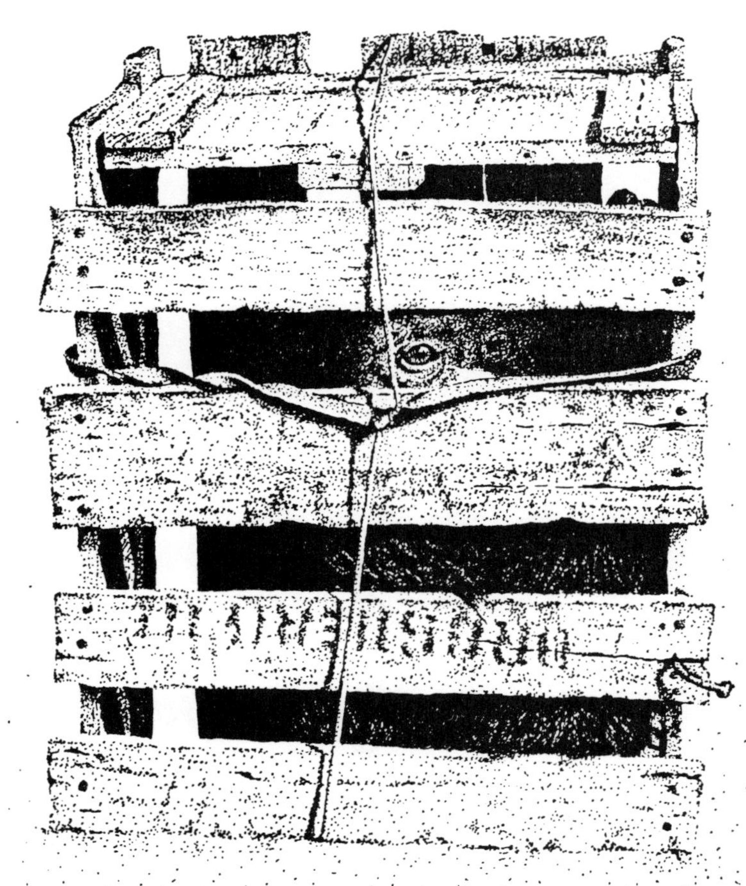

Manichean Geography I

Imagine a coral or guano atoll
Where a breezy Union Jack
Flaps above the police station.

There is a rusting mission hut
Built out of flattened tin cans
(Bully beef, beans and tomato pilchards)

Where the Reverend Bungo Buller
And his prophet, Joe Gimlet,
Preach the gospel of cargoes.

They worship a white god
Of dentures and worn toothbrushes
Who will come to earth, Hallelulia,

In a reconditioned Flying Fortress
Bearing bales of fresh calico
And a crate of Black and Deckers.

Seeding like brisk parachutes,
The ancestral spirits will fall
From the pod of an airship,

And the chosen people will serve
Themselves with orange jube-jubes
In a brand new discount warehouse.

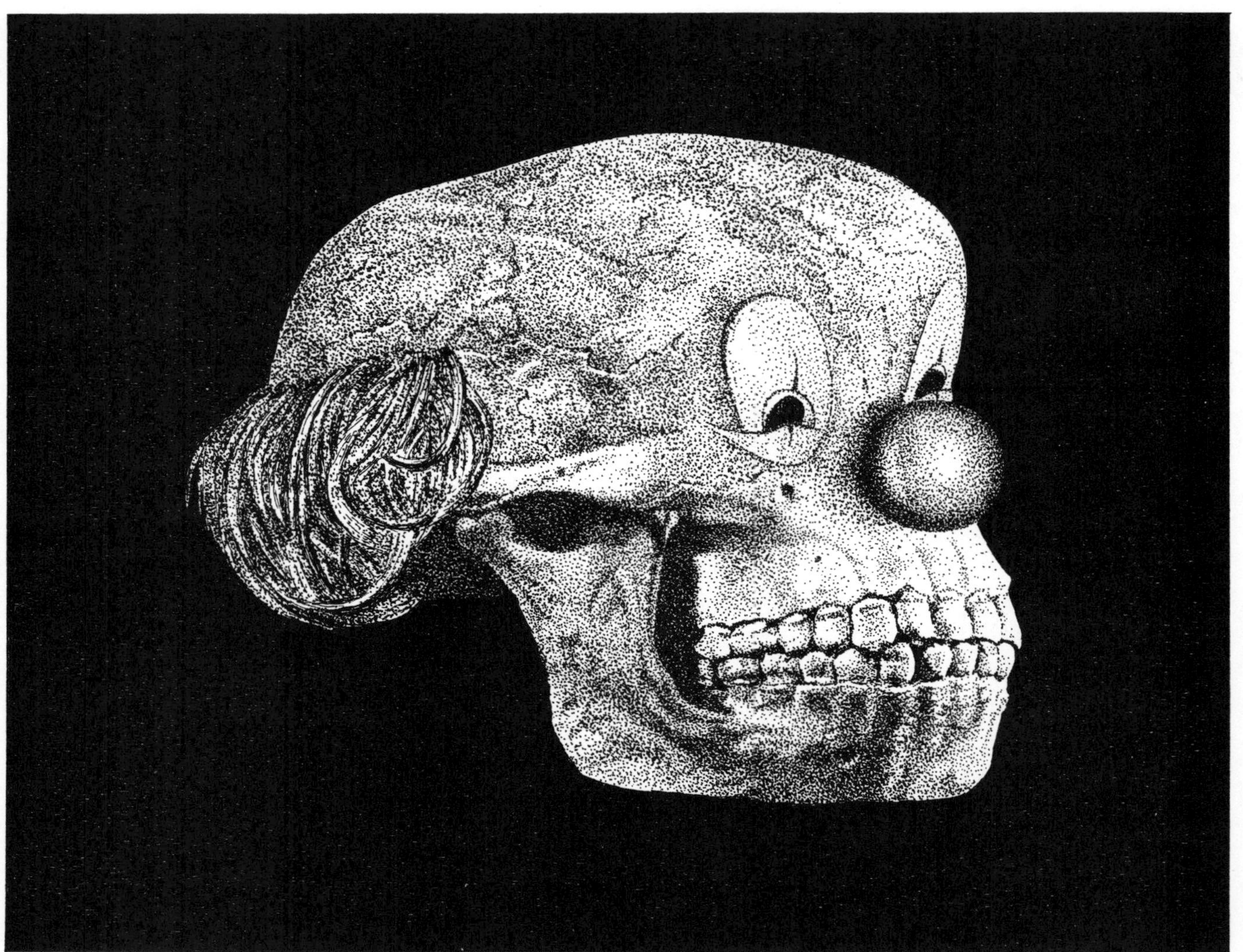

Manichean Geography II

Banal hours in muggy weather.
The slack wind—warm, trammelled –
Is named for a freighter
That dumped its clotted chains
In Prince Darling Bay.
One time, sometime, never again old chug.

From a rainwood pulpit
The Reverend Spanner McTavish
Preaches a burnt sermon
On the injustice of the Copra Board
While an Anglican head-hunter
Reads *Phrenology Made Easy*
And fidgets with his namba.
One time, sometime, never again old chug.

Sunset and a frigate-bird
Circling the chalk lighthouse.
In a twilight of flying foxes
The coconut crabs are shredding
'O' level papers in English Literature,
As a pidgin ode is chanted
In the deepy rainforest
To a signed photograph
Of His High Troppo Majesty
The Duke of Edinburgh.
One time, sometime, never again old chug.

To bossy saltmen from wayback
The islands are a kitsch necklace
Of prickly heat, boils,
And terminal yawns.
Big Ben Man, where is?
Asks the girl whose white teeth
Have the blank snowy dazzle
Of coconut flesh.
Just look what we've made
Of your damned islands, we answer.
They are images now
– Never again old chug –
Images of our own disgust.

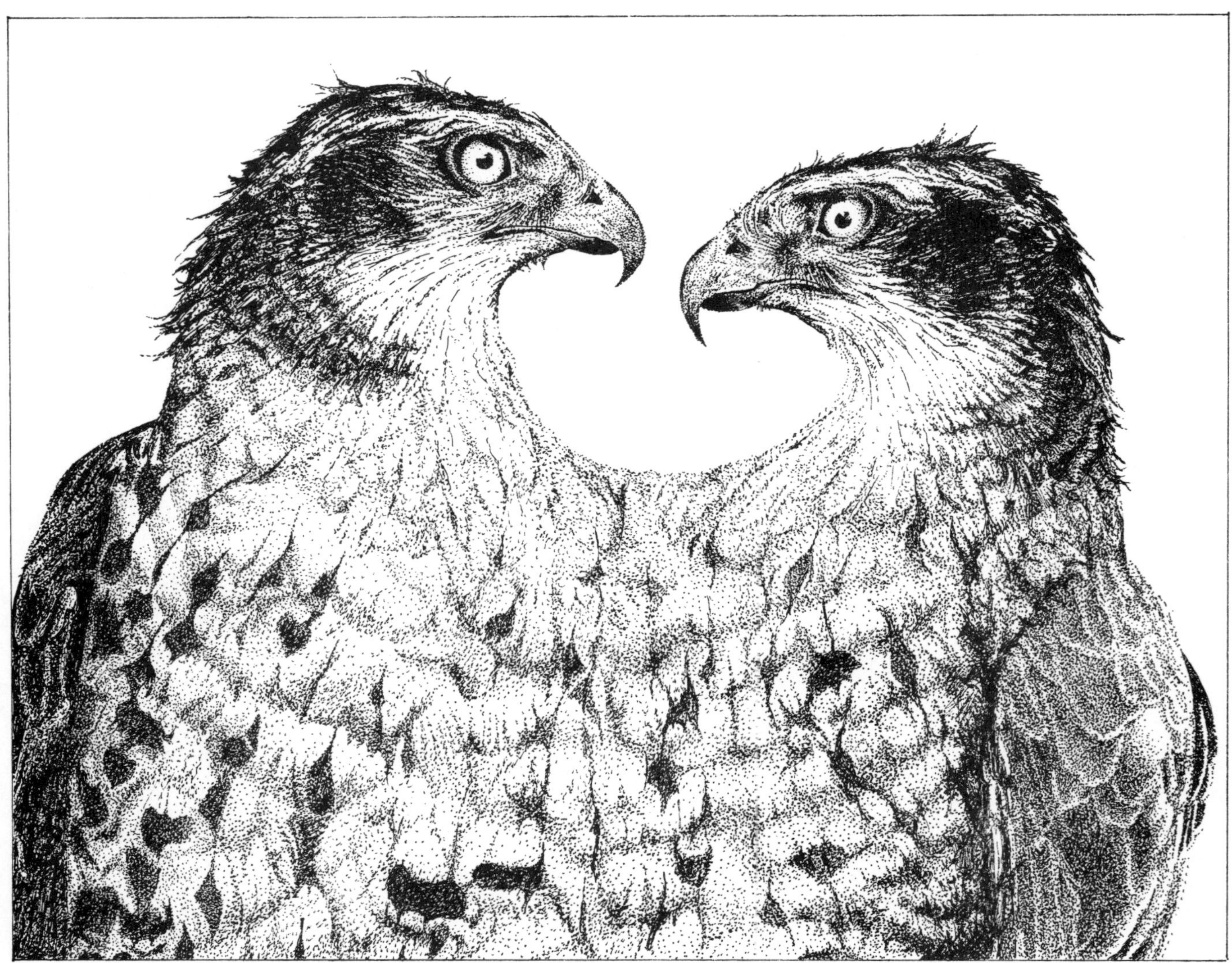

Desertmartin

At noon, in the dead centre of a faith,
Between Draperstown and Magherafelt.
This bitter village shows the flag
In a dry absolute September light.
Here, the Word has withered to a few
Parched certainties, and the charred stubble
Tightens like a black belt, a crop of bibles.

Because this is the territory of the Law
I drive across it with a powerless knowledge –
The owl of Minerva in a hired car.
A Jock squaddy glances down the street
And grins, happy and expendable,
Like a brass cartridge. He is a useful thing,
Almost at home, and yet not quite, not quite.

It's a limed nest, this place. I see a plain
Presbyterian grace sour, then harden,
As a free strenuous spirit changes
To a servile defiance that whines and shrieks
For the bondage of the letter: it shouts
For the Big Man to lead his wee people
To a clean white prison, their scorched tomorrow.

Masculine Islam, the rule of the Just,
Egyptian sand dunes and geometry,
A theology of rifle-butts and executions:
These are the places where the spirit dies.
And now, in Desertmartin's sandy light,
I see a culture of twigs and bird-shit
Waving a gaudy flag it loves and curses.

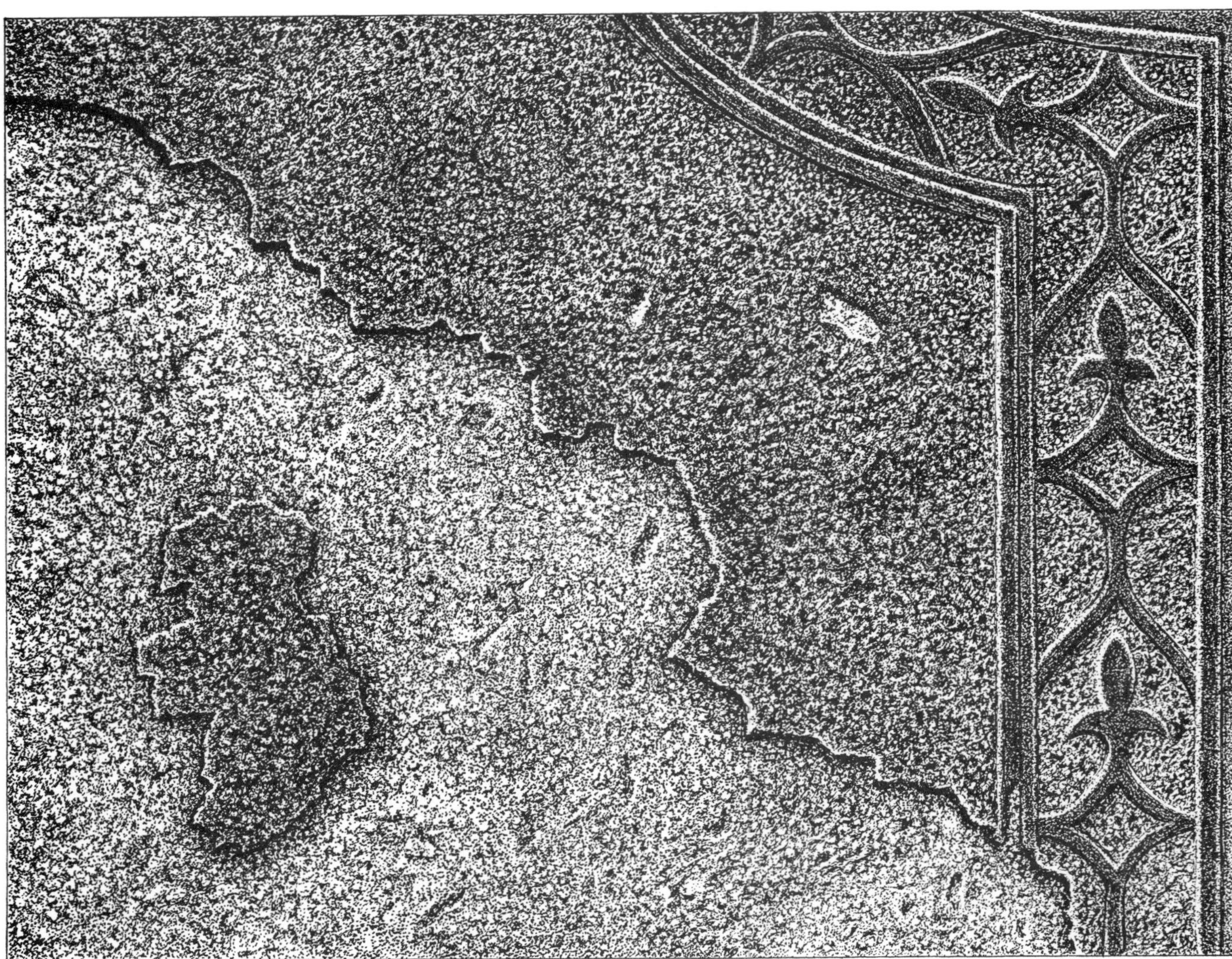

The Book of Juniper

In the original liturgy
on a bare island

a voice seeks an answer
in the sea wind:

'The tides parted and I crossed
barefoot to Inishkeel.

Where was the lost crozier
among the scorched bracken?

And where was that freshet
of sweet water?

Goose-grass and broken walls
were all my sanctuary,

I mistook a drowsed hour
for the spirit's joy;

on a thymy headland
I entered

the strict soul
of a dry cricket.

Heat haze and wild flowers,
a warm chirring all

that civil afternoon,
till its classic song

failed me and I sighed
for a different love

in grey weather.'

*

'Place the yeasty word
between my lips,

give me comfort
in a sheepfold,

shelter me
in a mild grove.'

*

'There is no word
and no comfort.

Only a lichened stone
is given you,

and juniper,
green juniper.'

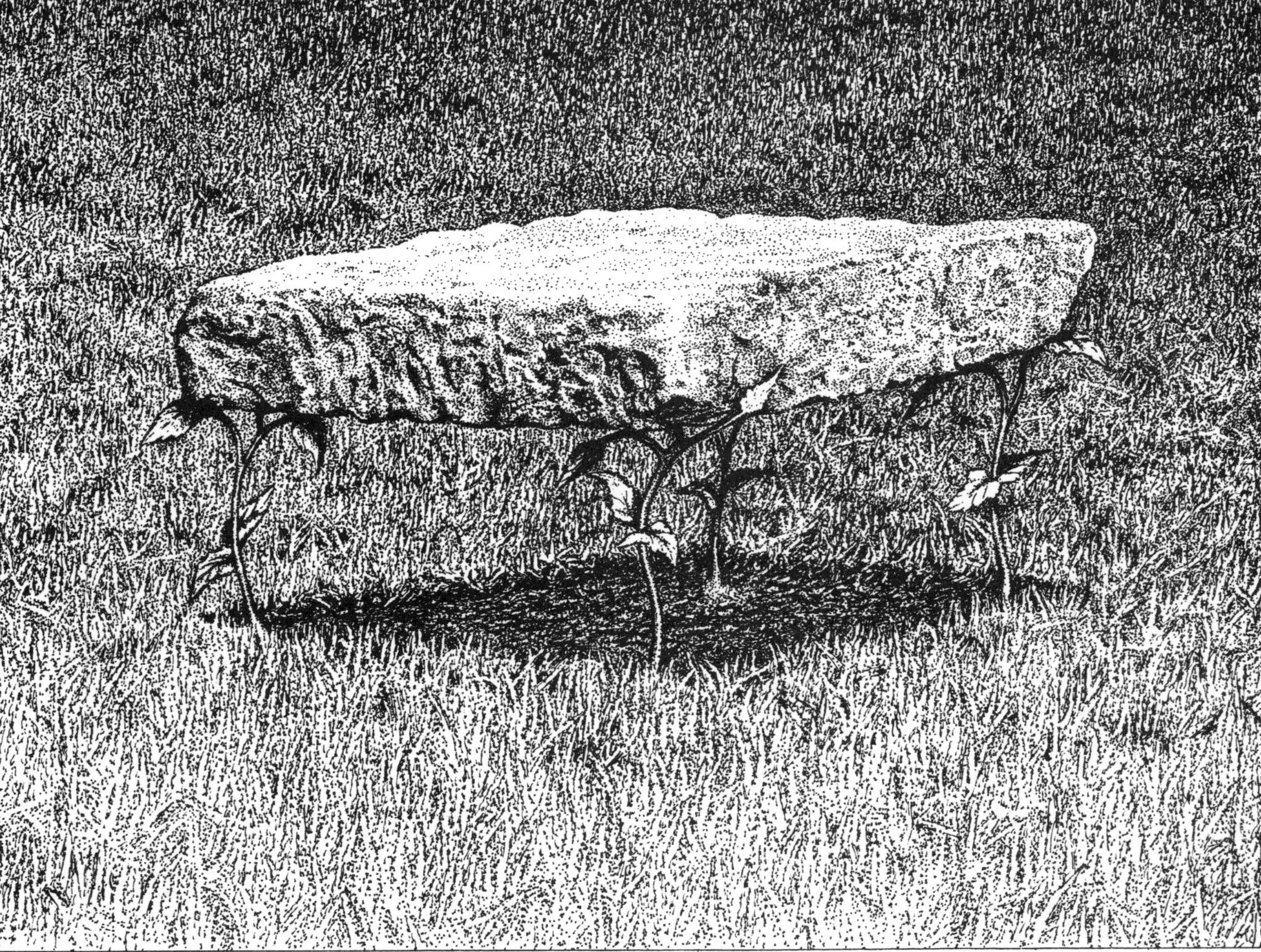

Tougher than the wind
it keeps a low profile
on rough ground.
Rugged, fecund,
with resined spines,
the gymnosperm
hugs the hillside
and wills its own survival.
The subtle arts are still to happen
and in the eye of a needle
a singing voice
tells a miniature epic
of the boreal forest:
not a silk tapestry
of fierce folk
warring on the tundra
or making exquisite love
on a starry counterpane,
but an in-the-beginning
was a wintry light
and *juniperus*.

*

On the brown hills
above a Roman spa
in Austro-Hungaria
the savin hides
its berries of blue wax
in a thorny crown,

while in the rapt
shaded casino
a small black ball
skips and ricochets
like a sniper's bullet.

Jug-ears and jowls,
walrus moustaches, frowns,
those gravid urns
on clotted mahogany.
What mineral water can soothe
a tetchy liver or a glum colon?

The wheel spins,
the hard pea itches,
sexual risk and riches
impress wives and mistresses
for an absolute moment
on a plush mattress.

Later, the dry scrape
of an empty tumbler
locked on a ouija board
will spell out a dead yes
like chalk on a billiard cue.

The wind riffles the savin;
the humid band begins to play.

*

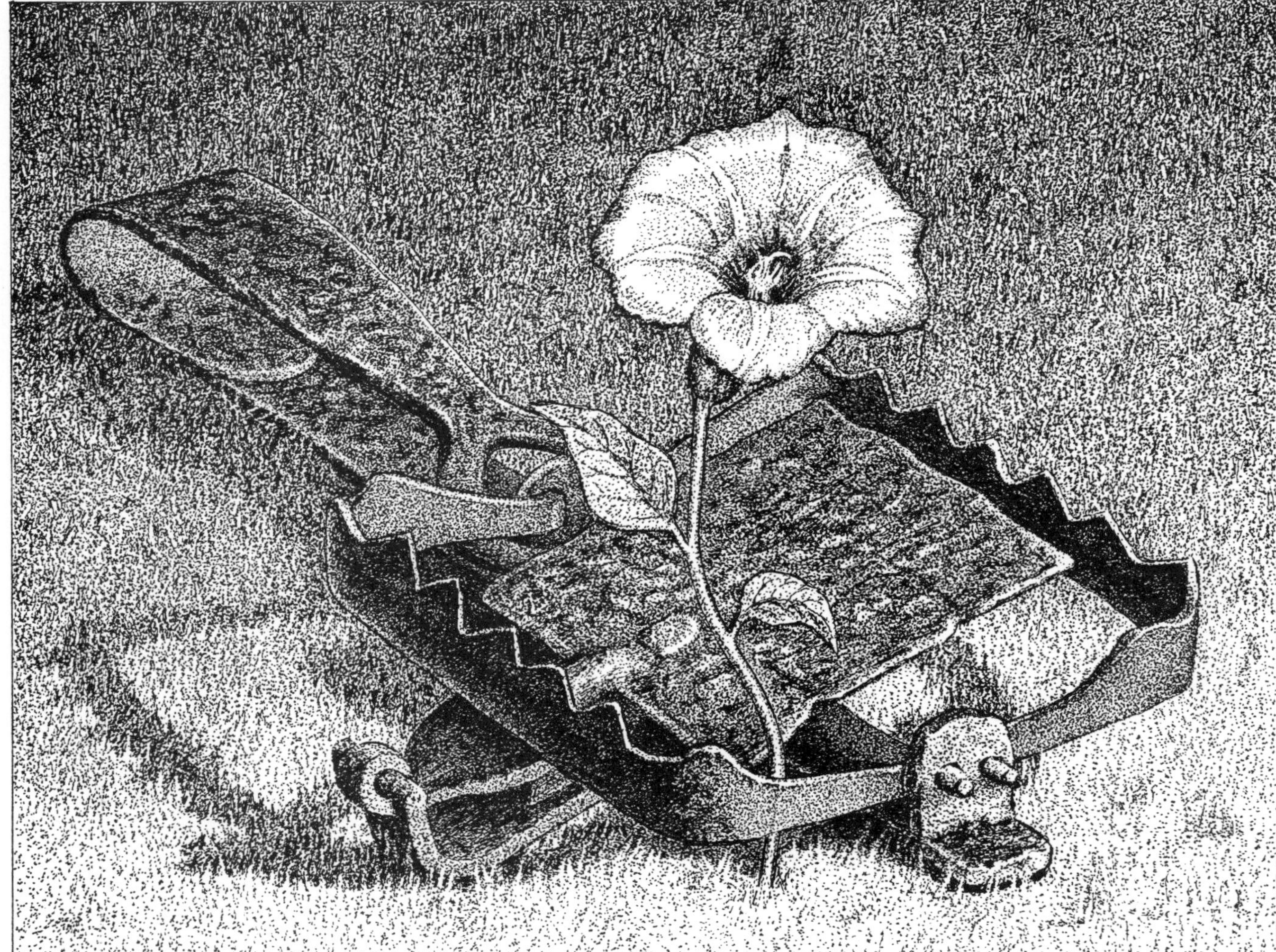

A clear and tearful fluid,
the bittersweet genièvre
is held to a wet window
above a college garden.

On the lazy shores
of a tideless sea,
the Phoenician juniper
burns a fragrant incense
in a sandy nest.

And in a Zen garden
all the miniature trees
have the perfect despair
of bound feet.

Exiled in Voronezh
the leavening priest of the Word
receives the Host on his tongue –
frost, stars, a dark berry,
and the sun is buried at midnight.

*

On a bruised coast
I crush a blue bead
between my fingers,
tracing the scent, somewhere,
of that warm mnemonic haybox,
burnished fields, a linen picnic,
and a summer dawn
where mushrooms rise among the stubble.
They are white in the dew
and this nordic grape
whets an eager moment
of naked passion and shrill light.
Its meek astringency is distilled
into perfume and medicines,
it matches venison
as the sour gooseberry
cuts the oily mackerel.
Spicy, glaucous,
its branches fan out
like the wind's shadow
on long grass,
then melt back
and go to ground
where swart choughs
open their red beaks,
stinging the air
with stony voices.

*

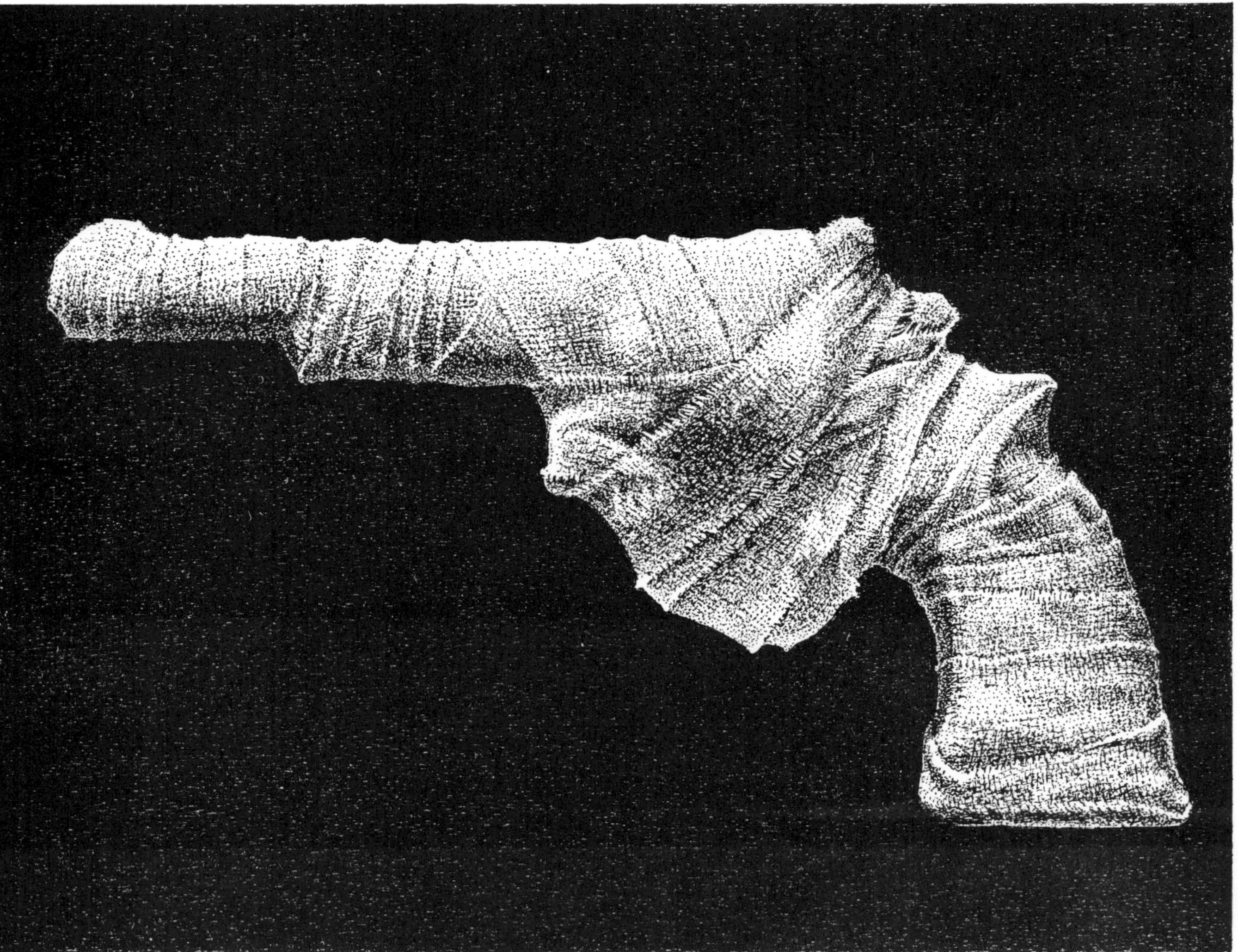

Though it might be a simple
decoration
or a chill fragrance
in a snug souterrain,
I must grasp again
how its green
springy resistance
ducks its head down and skirts
the warped polities of other trees
bent in the Atlantic wind.
For no one knows
if nature allowed it
to grow tall
what proud grace
the juniper tree might show
that flared, once, like fire
along the hills.

Consider
the gothic zigzags
and brisk formations
that square to meet
the green tide rising
through Mayo and Antrim,

now dream
of that sweet
equal republic
where the juniper
talks to the oak,
the thistle,
the bandaged elm,
and the jolly jolly chestnut.

*

On this coast
it is the only
tree of freedom
to be found,
and I imagine
that a swelling army is marching
from Memory Harbour and Killala
carrying branches
of green juniper.

Biographical Notes

TOM PAULIN was born in 1949. He has published two books of poems, *A State of Justice* (1977) and *The Strange Museum* (1980), both from Faber. His critical study *Thomas Hardy: the Poetry of Perception* was published by Macmillan in 1975.

NOEL CONNOR was born in Belfast in 1954. Exhibitions of his work have been held in Newcastle upon Tyne, Middlesbrough, London and Belfast. His drawings have appeared in various publications, including *The Honest Ulsterman, Iron, Poetry Review, Stand,* and the *Times Literary Supplement.* In 1979 Sunderland Press issued *In the Egyptian Gardens*, a poem-print collaboration with Tom Paulin (now reissued by Bloodaxe as a poster—see below), and Charlotte Press published *Gravities*, a collection of poems by Seamus Heaney with drawings by Connor. His latest project, *Wall*, is a collaboration between several artists and poets; it was published by the LYC Gallery, Brampton, Cumbria to coincide with an exhibition in May 1981.

IN THE EGYPTIAN GARDENS

A poem poster collaboration between Paulin and Connor first editioned as a print by Sunderland Press in 1979. The poster (reproduced opposite) measures 35cm x 48cm, and is printed in black on 170gsm Huntsman Velvet paper. Price £2.00 (+ 50p p&p).

Acknowledgements

Acknowledgements are due to the editors of the following publications in which these poems first appeared: *Encounter*, *New Statesman*, *Quarto*, *Poetry Supplement* (Poetry Book Society, Christmas 1979), *Times Literary Supplement*, and *The Writers: A Sense of Ireland*, ed. Andrew Carpenter & Peter Fallon (The O'Brien Press, Dublin, 1980).

    The poems 'Cinnamon Stick', 'Ceremony on the Border' and 'As a White Lodge in a Garden of Cucumbers' were printed with their drawings in *Poetry Review*.

Noel Connor gratefully acknowledges the financial assistance of Northern Arts.

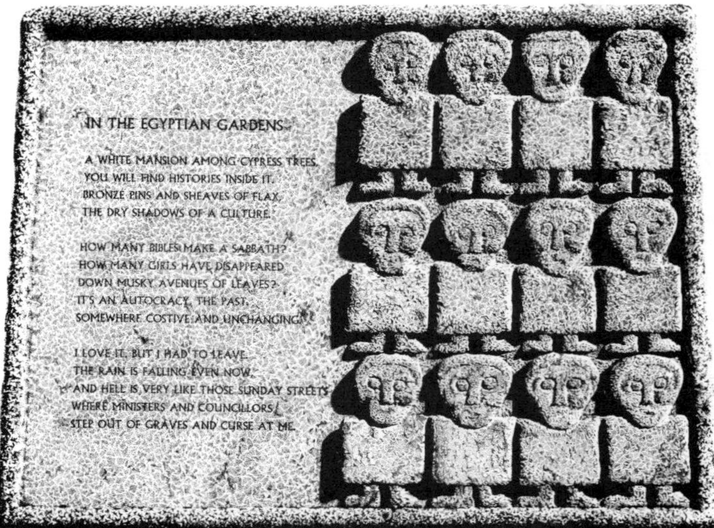